The Promise and Perils of Technology™

INTERNET SECURITY
AND YOU

Sherri Mabry Gordon

Rosen
YA

Published in 2020 by The Rosen Publishing Group, Inc.
29 East 21st Street, New York, NY 10010

Library of Congress Cataloging-in-Publication Data

Names: Gordon, Sherri Mabry, author.
Title: Internet security and you / Sherri Mabry Gordon.
Description: First edition. | New York, NY : The Rosen Publishing Group, Inc., 2020. |
Series: The promise and perils of technology | Includes bibliographical references and
index. | Audience: Grades 7 to 12.
Identifiers: LCCN 2018044836 | ISBN 9781508188285 (library bound) |
ISBN 9781508188278 (pbk.)
Subjects: LCSH: Computer crimes—Juvenile literature. | Internet—Security measures—
Juvenile literature. | World Wide Web—Security measures—Juvenile literature.
Classification: LCC HV6773 .G677 2020 | DDC 005.8—dc23
LC record available at https://lccn.loc.gov/2018044836

Manufactured in the United States of America

CONTENTS

Introduction 4

1   A Closer Look at Internet Security 6

2   The Dangers of the Internet 16

3   What You Need to Do to Protect Yourself 24

4   Hacked! What to Do If It Happens to You 34

5   What the Future Holds for Internet Security 42

Glossary. 50
For More Information 53
For Further Reading 56
Bibliography 57
Index 61

You may have never experienced a life without the internet. In fact, you may have never known a life that didn't offer information, music, and movies all at the click of a button. Although you may not be able to imagine a world without smartphones and laptops, surprisingly, the World Wide Web, which people use to access the internet, is not even thirty years old. Since its inception, it has made people's lives so much easier—and so much more connected.

But with this connectivity comes a price. With each technological advance comes additional opportunities for cybercriminals and hackers to have immediate access to your life. In fact, the speed at which information passes from one person to another is frightening. Although this speed makes it great for streaming videos and music, it also makes it extremely easy for hackers to access your personal data quickly and efficiently, especially if you have not taken steps to protect yourself.

It's important to realize that absolute safety while on the internet is simply not possible. As technological advances are made, it will become increasingly difficult to keep your personal information, such as passwords, Social Security numbers, addresses, birthdates, and credit card numbers private. No matter what you are doing online, your information is not only being mined, but also is at risk for theft.

The internet has made people's lives easier than in previous decades. For instance, in the past, people used to write letters and then wait for a response. Today, they can send text messages and emails with just the click of a button.

This resource will share with you the countless risks you face every time you get online. But more importantly, it will show you how to keep your data as safe as possible. And, if you are hacked, there are tips for handling that, too. The key is to stay vigilant when using the internet. Because if you do, you can attain a reasonable level of internet security.

A Closer Look at Internet Security

Some have called it the hack of the century. Others have said it was an unprecedented attack on the gaming industry. But regardless of what it is called, when Sony's PlayStation Network (PSN) was attacked in April 2011, the hack left PSN's customers shocked and angry.

To make matters worse, Sony delayed telling consumers exactly what had happened even after the company quietly pulled PSN offline two days after the attack. Instead, Sony's communications were vague and customers speculated that the outage was just a system malfunction that would take forty-eight hours to repair. What they never imagined was that it would be another three weeks before the network would be online again—and that their privacy and personal data had been significantly compromised.

When word finally broke that personal information had indeed been stolen, gamers around the world were furious. Not only had Sony's internet security features failed, but the company had waited an entire week before making customers aware of the breach. Moreover, it was no small breach of security. In fact, Sony confirmed that users' names, home addresses, email addresses, birthdays, passwords, and usernames were in the hands of criminals—everything someone needed to steal a person's money or even their identity. Additionally, their PSN purchase history, profile data, and security questions also were at risk. Even credit card data was at risk. There was no doubt that PSN customers had been fully exposed.

When Sony's PlayStation Network was breached, people thought that the system was being serviced or had a small glitch that needed to be fixed. Little did they know that their privacy had been violated and all their personal information had been stolen.

Even worse, consumers were unable to alter the details of their PSN accounts to protect themselves because the system remained offline. Their only option was to change passwords on other accounts, cancel credit cards, and change security questions. When it was all said and done, some estimates indicated that hackers stole as many as seventy-seven million personal accounts. They also erased data from Sony's systems. They even stole private documents and prerelease movies and made them available to the public. It was an attack that would cost Sony more than $250 million by some estimates.

"On the gaming side, nothing like the PlayStation Network attack had happened before, or has happened since," Lewis Ward, a researcher for the gaming industry, told *Fortune* magazine. "It was unprecedented in gaming."

Meanwhile, Joseph Steinberg, a cybersecurity expert and contributor to *Forbes* magazine, believes poor internet security practices are to blame for the breach. He writes, "Some of the documents leaked ... show that Sony employees were using weak passwords and that poor data management policies were in place." The company also was not prepared for phishing attacks. And they likely did not practice proper use of encryption, data storage, and backups.

Experts speculate that the attack originated when a Sony employee clicked on a link in an email that compromised his system. Then, attackers sought out and stole private material and information. According to Gary Miliefsky, the chief executive officer (CEO) of a cybersecurity firm who was interviewed for the *Fortune* article, "The biggest weakness at Sony ... was the employees. If you can't train them to behave better, then what can you expect but another successful breach?"

For this reason, Steinberg stresses that consumers understand that any website, shopping network, or online system they are using could be practicing poor data management policies. As a result, you need to learn to protect yourself as much as you possibly can.

"Sophisticated attackers can inflict serious harm if you are not proactively vigilant with [personal data] and information security," Steinberg writes in *Forbes*. "Don't make it easy for them."

What Is Internet Security?

Thanks to the internet, people around the world are more connected than ever. Teens are especially connected because they spend a good amount of their time online. But most teens fail to consider that they are at risk while online. In fact, many assume that phishing, malware, and other attacks are things that impact only the business world or adults. In reality, though, teens experience the effects of these attacks every day through computer viruses, ransomware, and identity theft. An average of half a million kids have their identities stolen every year, according to Robert Chappell Jr., author of *Child Identity Theft: What Every Parent Needs to Know*.

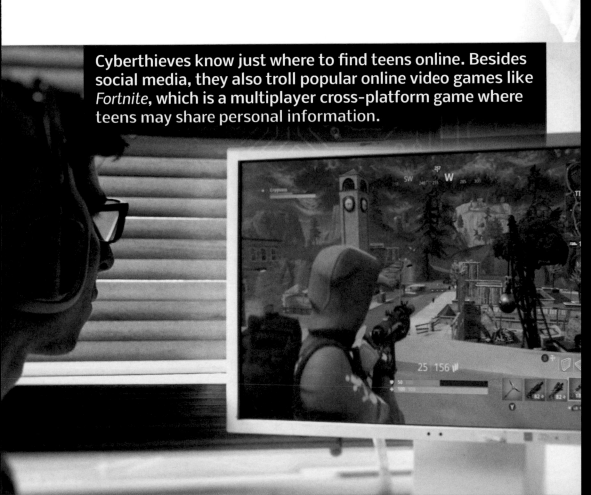

Cyberthieves know just where to find teens online. Besides social media, they also troll popular online video games like *Fortnite*, which is a multiplayer cross-platform game where teens may share personal information.

This theft happens because cyberthieves know where to find teens—in the places online where they spend a lot of their time—on social media, video streaming sites, and online video games. What's more, teens sometimes make good targets, especially if they are overly trusting and not knowledgeable about internet security.

So, what exactly is internet security? Overall, internet security is the process of making sure that all incoming and outgoing data or information from your computer is secure while you are on the internet. People often think that internet security applies just to browser security. But really it is more about network security. Internet security protects and authenticates every piece of information sent over the internet. Whether you are making a credit card purchase on Amazon or creating a personal profile on Instagram, all the information you send over the internet should be protected with

When people shop online, they are sharing personal data over the internet, including their address, phone number, email, and even credit card numbers. It is important to realize that anytime you share information online there could be someone out there trying to steal it or intercept it.

internet security procedures. But you can't just rely on the company's site you are using to keep your information safe. You also have to take steps to make sure your data and personal information is as secure as possible.

Remember, the internet is not a secure place to be, but it was never intended to be. When the internet was first conceived, it was designed as a loosely linked computer network that would allow people to share ideas and information freely. As a result, whether you are sending an email, shopping online, or writing a paper in Google Docs, data is being sent over the internet. Anytime this activity happens, hackers and scam artists have plenty of opportunities to intercept, change, or steal this information.

For this reason, it is extremely important that you know how to keep your data as safe and secure as possible. When you are proactive and stay educated about cybersecurity risks, then chances are good that you will stay safer online than other, less informed teens might.

Understanding the Types of Threats You Face

Anytime you go online, you are exposed to cybercriminals—people who commit fraud, steal people's identities, or harass others in some way. Although you may never have direct contact with these people, you need to know they are always there lurking in the shadows. Consequently, when you connect to the internet—whether it is at home, at school, at work, or at the local coffee shop—you need to make smart decisions that provide you with appropriate cybersecurity.

You need to be astute about cybersecurity and know what threats you are facing. You also need to use the right tools to stay as safe as possible online. Some experts compare internet security to that of driving a car. Although it takes a little practice and an understanding of the possible risks, you are eventually able to control the car and take it safely where you want to go. The same is true about the internet.

Three Internet Security Myths Debunked

Myth 1: Installing antivirus software is enough.

In the 1990s, antivirus software might have been sufficient, but in today's sophisticated digital world, it is only one layer of protection. Hackers have found multiple ways to get around antivirus software and often hide their attacks within the system. With ransomware on the market today, the amount of time between infection and damage is almost instantaneous. As a result, you need to develop a prevention mindset that questions almost everything that is requested of you or offered online.

Myth 2: The chances of me experiencing a data breach are small.

Believing that it will never happen to you is almost a guarantee that it will. In fact, the more vulnerable you are online— such as having weak passwords, sharing too much information, and not updating your software— the greater the chance you are going to be exploited. For example, a report developed by Verizon found that 63 percent of data breaches were the result of weak or stolen passwords. Meanwhile, a study by CompTIA found that human error accounted for 52 percent of internet security breaches. People make mistakes. For this reason, you need to be vigilant about protecting yourself anytime you are online. If you are not careful, a breach could very well happen to you.

Myth 3: Visiting a website won't hurt me as long as I don't do anything.

Many people believe that you have to actually do something on a rogue website to be infected. But that is not the case. Hackers have developed what are sometimes called drive-by websites, where simply loading the page infects your computer. Additionally, links to these websites are often disguised in emails, texts, and direct messages that appear to be from friends. To someone not paying attention, it is easy to click on a link to a drive-by website. Firewalls often can't detect these dangerous sites, especially if they are part of normal internet traffic. As a result, you need to be extremely cautious about visiting websites with which you are unfamiliar.

One aspect that will help you navigate the information superhighway safely is understanding the types of threats you are facing online. Basically, there are two distinct types of threats. These include undirected threats and directed threats. Most of the threats you will face are automated undirected threats. Fortunately, these also are the easiest to defend against.

In general, undirected threats are not aimed at you personally but still might have an impact on you. Some examples include phishing emails and computer viruses. Unprotected websites can be dangerous as well, especially if you supply credit card information and other personal data. To protect yourself from undirected threats, you need to practice general internet safety guidelines, including strong passwords, secure emails, and secure browsing.

Meanwhile, directed threats are more dangerous and typically aimed at you personally or an organization you are affiliated with. In addition, directed threats often involve a lot of different techniques.

Phishing emails and computer viruses are examples of undirected threats. They are not aimed at you personally but are still dangerous. To protect yourself from these threats, you need to make sure you have strong passwords and use secure browsing.

For instance, attackers might use a mix of social engineering, phishing, malware, and more. Directed attacks are also a lot more expensive to address. One source of directed threats comes from foreign governments. Their goals often range from extorting money and shutting down services to creating havoc for their targets.

Remember that cyberattacks, whether directed or undirected, can rob you of your personal data, your money, and even your identity. To prevent this loss from happening to you, it is important to take internet security seriously. You can avoid risks by being smart, understanding what might happen if you click or share, and making wise choices.

"[Although] you will never be 100 percent safe as long as you are on the internet, you can reach a point where you're as safe as you reasonably need to be," writes Eric Ravenscraft on Lifehacker. "While it's tempting to get worried or scared when you hear about a looming conspiracy or company that got hacked, just remember that online security isn't just about having the strongest lock. It's also about using the right tools for the job and knowing when to take your data offline."

The Dangers of the Internet

I t was Cassidy Wolf's worst nightmare. Someone had hacked into her laptop and had been spying on her for more than a year. During that time, the hacker took screenshots of her changing clothes and going back and forth from the shower. After amassing a collection of photos, he then demanded through an email that she do what he said or he would share everything.

"When I first read the email from my hacker, I couldn't stop screaming," Cassidy recalls to Julia Rubin of Teen Vogue. "I didn't know what to do; I was in a state of complete shock and terror. [When I received a notification that someone had tried to change my Facebook password while at dinner with friends], I sensed something was wrong, but this [email from him] was my horrifying confirmation."

Fortunately, Cassidy called her mom right away, who got the police involved. Eventually, the Federal Bureau of Investigation (FBI) took over the investigation. But the next three months while the investigation was taking place, were excruciating. The hacker sent nearly thirty emails each day until the authorities caught him.

Cassidy says she must have opened an email and clicked on the link that enabled the hacker, later identified as Jared James Abrahams, to install malware, or software that is created to damage or gain unauthorized control of a computer. This malicious software enabled him to capture the keystrokes on her laptop's keyboard and discover her passwords. He also could find out what websites she visited, and he could access her webcam anytime he wanted. This capability is how he stockpiled a huge collection of photos of her.

Investigators were eventually able to track him down using emails, IP addresses, and other communications. They also tied him to online forums where he had asked about malware, how to control webcams, and details on hacking into Facebook accounts.

"[This] could happen to anybody," Cassidy says in Teen Vogue. "[Now] … I constantly change my passwords, and I never log into my accounts at friends' houses. And, of course, I no longer open emails from people I don't know."

Why Internet Security Is Important

After being named Miss California Teen and Miss Teen USA, Cassidy Wolf made it her mission to educate others about the importance of internet security.

Most people cannot go long without doing something on the internet. Whether it is checking social media, reading the news, responding to emails, researching a paper, shopping for music or clothes, or completing online banking transactions, people use the internet every day. When they do, they share lots of personal data on the sites they visit.

Internet security is not just an issue that affects adults. With cases like Cassidy's in the news every day, it becomes painfully obvious why

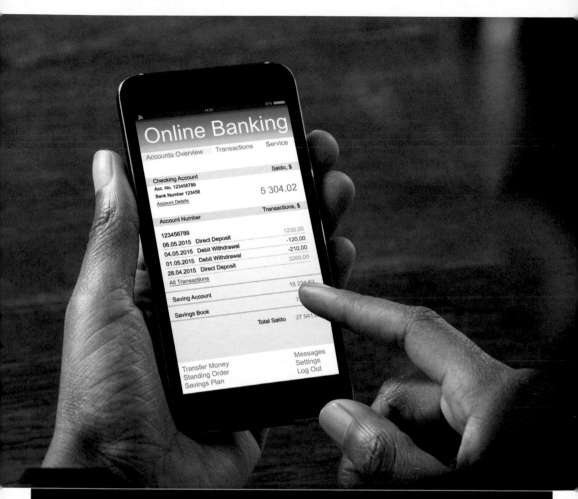

Online banking is very convenient and saves time, but it also can put your privacy at risk. To protect yourself, consider setting up alerts on your account, which will let you know when your password has been changed or when a significant withdrawal has taken place.

internet security is an issue that teens need to be aware of, too. Daily, hackers are spying on them, stealing their personal information, impersonating them online, and stealing their money.

In fact, data breaches are a growing problem across the globe with no end in sight. According to a recent Internet Security Report published by Symantec, nearly half a billion personal records were stolen or lost in 2015 alone. As the internet continues to evolve and computer networks become bigger, the need for security is going to grow as well.

Just How Important Is Privacy and Security to Americans?

According to the Pew Research Center, Americans feel that online privacy is important. Yet, according to the report, many feel they do not have much control over data that is collected about them or how it is used. They also have extremely low confidence in the companies that have their personal information and worry they are not keeping it safe.

For instance, just 6 percent of people say they are "very confident" that government agencies can keep their records private and secure. Meanwhile, only 9 percent have a high level of confidence that credit card companies keep their data private and secure. Online service providers instill the least amount of confidence in their consumers, with 76 percent of people saying they are not too confident that their information is secure.

Yet, very few people have changed their behavior to keep their data more secure. According to Pew, 91 percent of people had not made any changes to their internet or cellphone use. Clearly, Americans need to be taking more steps to manage the online risks they face every day.

How Do Security Breaches Happen?

Most of the time, a security breach occurs because of human error somewhere along the way. Someone opens an email, clicks on a link, and unintentionally installs malicious software that contains viruses, worms, Trojan horses, and other harmful software. Other times, they will forget to secure their computer or their workstation, which makes them an easy target for potential attackers. Still others give sensitive information to outsiders without even realizing it. All these things can lead to a data breach.

There are a number of tools that hackers use to gain control and get the information they want. Here is an overview of some of the ways in which hackers can compromise internet security and gain access.

Social engineering. This tactic is the art of manipulating people into giving up confidential information. Usually, the information they are after includes money, bank account numbers, Social Security numbers, and passwords. Sometimes they will pretend to be a reputable company to gain access to your information. Other times, they will pretend to be a friend who needs help. When hackers make these types of requests, this is called phishing. Never send confidential information through email or provide it to a source you have not verified first.

Eavesdropping. As one of the more common types of attacks, eavesdropping occurs when a hacker gains critical information by "listening" to network traffic. Many communications that take place online are not encrypted, so the traffic sent over the network can be

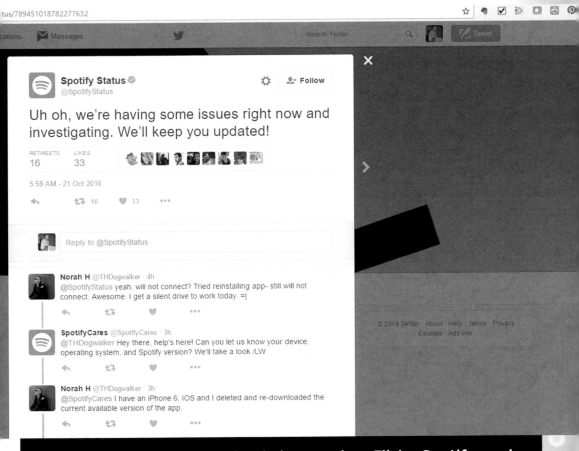

On October 21, 2016, several websites, such as Flickr, Spotify, and Etsy, had their services interrupted by a large-scale distributed denial of service (DDoS) attack. A DDoS attack is one that often causes a system to crash by making multiple requests.

analyzed and read. For this reason, you should never send highly confidential information on sites that are not secure.

DoS and DDoS attacks. Denial of service (DoS) and distributed denial of service (DDoS) attacks overwhelm a data system by making simultaneous requests to a website. DoS comes from a single source and DDoS comes from multiple sources. These attacks often cause the web server to crash or become inoperable when it tries to handle all the requests. In the end, the company's real users cannot access the website or its services.

Password attacks. These attacks are one of the most feared attacks to large organizations because once a password is cracked, the entire network can be damaged, especially if the password belongs to a network administrator. This risk is one of the reasons that companies use strong passwords that are changed frequently.

Application-layer attacks. These types of attacks are the most common and are based on cracking applications that run on servers or workstations. For instance, hackers use viruses, worms, or more to gain important information.

Exploit attacks. If a hacker has superior computing skills, he or she might execute an exploit attack, especially if the hacker has in-depth knowledge of particular software bugs. As a result, the hacker will exploit the problem and gain access to private data.

IP address spoofing. Spoofing is a type of cyberattack where a hacker attempts to use a computer, device, or network to trick other computer networks into believing it is a real entity. It is a common way for hackers to gain access to computers and mine them for personal data. They also might turn the computers into zombies or launch DoS attacks.

Ramifications of Poor Internet Security

When hackers manage to break into an organization's systems, website, or even your own computer, they can do a lot of damage. As Cassidy found out, they can take over your computer, hack into your accounts, and invade your privacy. Other ramifications include a loss of intellectual property; a ruined reputation; theft of money, identity and data; and a damaged computer.

Although cybersecurity is an important issue, no one is suggesting that you go off the grid to keep your information and your privacy intact. Even Cassidy, who gets a sick feeling in her stomach every time her cell phone chimes with an email notification, continues to use the internet. "I still use social media," she explains to Teen Vogue. "I initially deleted my Twitter and my Instagram, but have since gotten new accounts, and I've kept my Facebook. I like having them and being able to interact with my friends. I realized I had to live the way I always had, but now I'm super careful."

What You Need to Do to Protect Yourself

Ask any cybersecurity professional how to stay safe online and you will get a laundry list of do's and don'ts. But is there really a foolproof way to keep your data safe online? There answer is both yes and no. Most cybersecurity professionals will tell you that you and your data are never absolutely secure online. But there are things you can do to make it hard for hackers and other opportunists to steal your information. The key is to understand the risks and then take the proper precautions.

Knowing Where the Weak Spots Are

Because the internet is easily accessible to anyone in the world, it can be a very dangerous place. Everyone from predators and cybercriminals to bullies and corrupt organizations will try to take advantage of people who are not educated about the risks. As a result, it is important to know what you're up against every time you log on. Remember, your data is important and you never want to put it at risk. Once it is in the hands of the wrong person, it can be very hard to make your information secure again. Here's an overview of the top risks that teens face online.

Opening emails from people you don't know or clicking on links in an email. When using your email, it is always a good rule of thumb to exercise caution when opening emails that contain links. Too many times, clicking on these links is all a hacker needs to install malware into your computer or take control of your device.

As a result, never click on a link in an email, even if it is from someone you know. Remember, if your friend has been hacked, many times the hacker will send out emails to all contacts as a way of spreading their viruses and malicious software. Always verify that your friend sent you the link before clicking on it. Furthermore, you should never open an email from someone you do not know, and definitely do not click on any links that individual provides.

Failing to keep browsers and software up to date. Yes, it is annoying to get those notifications that updates are available for your smartphone or your laptop. But, you need to routinely update your software to ensure that you are not at risk for any known security threats. It also is really important to update your browser regularly. Remember, your browser is the doorway from your computer to the internet. So, keep it as secure as possible.

Thinking antivirus software is enough protection. Most people think that if they have antivirus software that is all they have to do to protect their computer. While good internet security software will immediately remove viruses, advise you when you're about to click on a malicious site, and regularly scan your computer for malicious software, it is not the only thing you need to be doing to protect yourself.

Using websites that are not secure or clicking on malicious websites. Secure websites have "https" at the beginning of the URL, instead of just "http." Although using sites with "https" does not mean that your information is absolutely secure, it does mean that the communications between your web browser and the website are encrypted. This encryption makes it difficult for hackers to intercept what you are typing, such as passwords, security questions, email addresses, payment information, and so on.

Downloading games, software, and videos without verifying. Cybercriminals often trick people into downloading malware. One

Protect yourself online by checking the website's URL before entering personal information. Websites beginning with "https" generally indicate that the website is secure.

way they do that is by convincing victims to download "games" or "videos." Before you download anything, be sure it is actually what it says it is. If you are not sure, ask your parents or another trusted adult. Offering free games or software is one way that hackers are able to gain access to your computer, steal your information, or hijack the device and use it as a botnet. Make sure you use legitimate ways to stream or download music and movies.

Storing information online when you don't have to. While it certainly makes online shopping easier to have your credit card information, address, and birthday all stored in an online account, doing so sets you up for theft, especially if hackers are able to breach the online retailer's system. Instead, opt not to store your information online, especially credit card information. Better yet, always check out as a guest.

How to Stay Cyber Safe

Just about everyone is online these days. Whether you are surfing the web, watching Netflix, or playing a game, you probably spend a lot of time connected. Therefore, it is very important that you take steps to manage your risks online. These risks include both technological risks and behavioral risks. With technological risks, your data is at risk because of dangerous software and bugs in the programs that are used. As for behavioral risks, these involve poor decisions that are made online.

Manage Your Technological Risks

Take steps not only to understand the software and hardware you are using, but also to learn how to take advantage of the built-in privacy and security tools. Doing so takes very little time and will help keep your time on the internet secure. Here are some ways you can reduce technological risks.

Secure your wireless network. You always want to be sure you have set a strong password or passphrase on your wireless router. Not only does this keep people outside of your house off your network, but it also helps prevent access to the devices on your network.

Stay safe in wireless hotspots. Many teens are always looking for free Wi-Fi. As a result, they often connect to a network without

Google May Be Putting Your Privacy at Risk

In January 2017, Google announced that its G Suite for Education—the selection of Google apps that includes Google Docs, Google Drive, and more—had seventy million users worldwide. Further, more than twenty million Chromebooks were in use in schools on a weekly basis. But some security experts worry that students' privacy may be at risk.

For instance, Google has admitted to data mining, or scanning millions of student emails that use G Suite for Education. They even had a complaint filed against them in federal court. Yet, they are still mining data from students. According to the Electronic Frontier Foundation (EFF), Google is collecting far

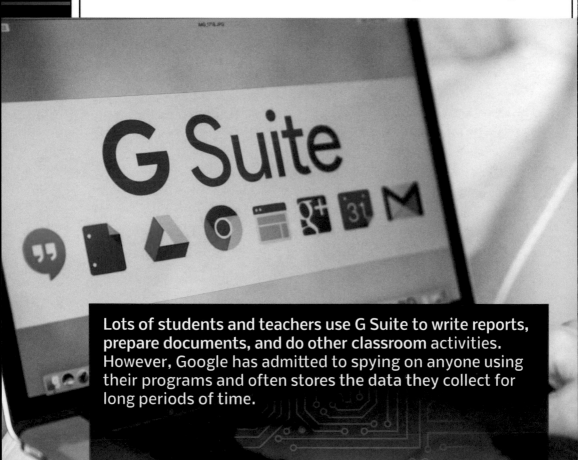

Lots of students and teachers use G Suite to write reports, prepare documents, and do other classroom activities. However, Google has admitted to spying on anyone using their programs and often stores the data they collect for long periods of time.

more information on kids than is necessary and is often storing that information indefinitely.

In addition to personally identifying information (PII) like name and date of birth, the information can include browsing history, search terms, location data, contact lists, and behavioral information. Sometimes this student data is even uploaded to the cloud automatically.

"In short, technology providers like Google are spying on students—and school districts, which often provide inadequate privacy policies or no privacy policy at all, are unwittingly helping them do it," writes Gennie Gebhart, one of the researchers at EFF, in a report, *Spying on Students: School-Issued Devices and Student Privacy.*

thinking about whether or not it is secure. Make sure you take the time to pick a secure network and the correct network. Picking a secure network means selecting the network with a lock next to it, whereas picking the correct network means you make sure that the spelling is correct for the network you are accessing. As added protection, set your devices to ask before they connect. This precaution will help you ensure that you are accessing a secure network. Finally, when you are using free Wi-Fi, avoid logging into accounts that require you to use your personal information like bank accounts and online shopping accounts.

Learn how to manage your firewall. Firewalls allow you to control data connections coming in to your network from other computers. Both Mac and Windows computers have built-in firewall capabilities. Be sure to use them.

Delete your cookies regularly. When you use different websites, cookies, or small files, are stored on your computer that track what you are doing. For instance, they might include your login

To teens, finding a Wi-Fi connection is always a plus. It means they do not have to use their own data or even their own equipment if they use a public computer. But there are risks with these scenarios, especially if they share personal or private information.

information, credit card information, and more. It is wise to delete this information consistently.

Update your software. As mentioned earlier, it is important to update your software on a consistent basis. Not doing so could put your data at risk. Many updates correct issues and bugs that may put your data in danger.

Use privacy tools. Many browsers and social media sites allow you to decide how much personal information you want to share with others. Take the time to set your privacy settings to the most secure settings.

Manage Your Behavioral Risks

From embarrassing comments and photos, to sharing too much personal information, the behavioral risks teens face every day are numerous. Because hackers are always on the lookout for an easy score, it is important to be smart about how you use the internet. Doing so will help you keep your personal data safe and secure. Here's an overview of the top things teens can do to keep their information safe online.

Select strong passwords or passphrases. Having a strong password or passphrase is a fundamental part of internet security. You also should avoid using the same password on multiple sites. If a hacker gets ahold of the password to your email and it is the same as your bank account, it becomes extremely easy for him to access everything. If you have trouble remembering all of your passwords, look into various password management systems. It's also important never to share your passwords with your friends. Doing so compromises your security and your safety.

Never give out personal information. Reputable companies will never ask you to send them account information or passwords by email. As a result, do not respond to phishing emails that request private information. Cybercriminals often pretend to be schools, banks, and other reputable organizations to get important information from teens.

Think before you click. When you are using the internet, always think before you click or post. This includes everything from clicking on links or attachments in emails to clicking Like on a social media post that is damaging or hurtful. Many times, these articles are just clickbait.

Do not blindly trust anything online. There are plenty of scams, fake news, and false information on the internet. Only visit reputable sites for news and health information and never download something from a site without first verifying that it is authentic. Use

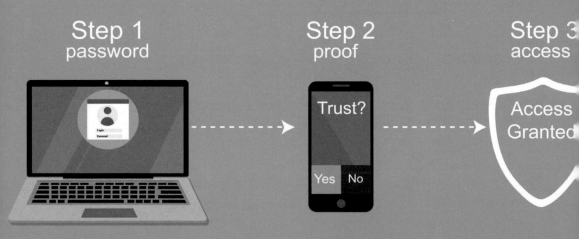

Sometimes setting a strong password is still not enough to keep your information safe. Therefore, some companies require two-factor authentication, in which a user will need to use both his or her phone and computer to log in.

a site such as the fact-checking site Snopes.com to verify claims that seem outrageous.

Consider using extra authentication. Some sites now offer multifactor authentication, which reduces the chance of unauthorized use. Typically, it requires you to take an extra step at log-in, but your information is more secure when you do. Usually, you will need to enter a code that is sent to your mobile phone to verify that you are the one using the account.

When it comes to the possibility of hacking, far too many teens suffer from the belief that "it won't happen to me." But experts predict that the number of teens hacked each day will continue to grow unless people learn how to be more proactive about their internet security. Make certain that you are taking the necessary steps to stay safe online.

Hacked! What to Do If It Happens to You

"You have been hacked!" Those four words strike fear into the heart of anyone with an online presence. Whether your personal data gets compromised in a Sony-style breach or your computer gets hacked and taken hostage, as in Cassidy's case, getting hacked is a nightmare. Knowing what to expect and how to fix it can help alleviate some of the stress. Then hopefully going forward, you can remain a little more protected.

Signs You Have Been Hacked

A smart hacker can break into your device, steal everything they can, and then leave without a trace. After all, their goal is not to get caught. So, many have learned stealthy ways to slip silently inside your device and leave a trail of destruction behind them. The end result for you is malware, weird pop-up ads, and sometimes even an empty bank account. Consequently, it is important that you know what to look for so that you can put an end to the attack. Here are some signs your laptop or smartphone has been compromised.

Your computer, smartphone, or tablet seems slower. When malware is running in the background, it can impact the performance of your software and apps. Malware transmissions also can slow down your device's network connection. Sometimes, though, a recent update can be the cause. Don't panic if your device is particularly slow.

If strange pop-ups or warnings show up on your computer or phone, they could indicate that the device has been infected with a virus. Even if the pop-ups are authentic, clicking on them could damage your device or allow a virus to be installed.

Your device is sending emails or messages that you did not create. If your family and friends start telling you that they are receiving weird messages from you, be sure to investigate right away. Likewise, if you start receiving strange emails, lots of spam, or strange texts, this could be a sign of a breach.

Warning !

** YOUR COMPUTER HAS BEEN BLOCKED **

Your computer has alerted us that it has been spyware. The following information is being s

> Facebook Login
> Credit Card Details
> Email Account Login

If your device suddenly stops working or is no longer allowing you to perform certain functions, it could be a sign that malware has been installed on your device.

Your device's battery is draining quickly, and it feels hotter than normal. Anytime extra code is running in the background, your battery is going to get depleted. Your device will feel extra hot to the touch because it is working so hard. For instance, malware that is running in the background, constantly monitoring and capturing your activity and then relaying it to another party, is going to be taxing on your device.

You start seeing pop-ups that never used to be present. Some malware produces a pop-up that asks the user to perform various functions. Typically, the pop-up looks like a real request from your system. Be cautious about clicking on these items. Even trying to close them out could infect your device.

You notice websites look different or apps are not working properly. Sometimes when malware has been installed, it sits between your browser and the internet. This situation is known as proxying. When this malware is proxying, it is reading the contents of all communications and maybe even sending instructions as well. This disruption in transmission is why things look different on your device or fail to work properly.

You experience service disruptions. If suddenly you start hearing strange noises on the line or have calls drop when you have strong service, this could be a sign that your device has been hacked. Under normal circumstances, these issues could be related to a technical glitch. But if you recently completed an action on your device that you are questioning, this also could be a sign that something is amiss.

What You Can Do

While being hacked appears to be getting increasingly common, it isn't getting any less confusing or stressful. In fact, it is often hard to know where to begin. Perhaps the best place to start is to ask yourself why this happened in the first place. Whether you were hacked, phished, or had malware installed, now is a good time to step back and ask yourself, "What was the reason behind this breach?" Knowing why it happened also can help you understand how you were breached—or where the attack is coming from. Here are some steps you need to take immediately.

Run a scan of your device. Even if you are pretty sure you have been hacked, it is always a good idea to scan your device, especially if you have antivirus software installed on your computer. If you do not have antivirus software, you can download Malwarebytes—a free antivirus software program—to scan your system. Sometimes though, there will be instances where a threat is not detected, or

Emotional Repercussions of Being Hacked

Experts say that being hacked can have a serious impact on your mental health. When hackers leaked nude photos of Jennifer Lawrence in 2014, she said it felt like a sexual violation. Meanwhile, other victims of hacking have gone as far as to commit suicide. Yet, companies often do not know how to deal with the emotional side of hacking, and victims are left picking up the pieces on their own.

The anxiety, stress, and trauma of experiencing a data breach can leave victims feeling powerless. According to an article by Nicole Kobie on Motherboard, a 2010 report by the security firm Norton says that victims feel frustrated and powerless because it seems unlikely that the cybercriminals will be brought to justice. The report also revealed that 58 percent of victims struggle with anger and 40 percent report feeling cheated.

The severity of the psychological effects depend on the nature of the attack, says Dr. Cassandra Cross, a senior lecturer at the Queensland University of Technology, who was quoted in Kobie's article. Waiting a long time to tell victims that a breach occurred also increases the psychological impact.

Cross says that cybercrime and its effects are not going away anytime soon. "Ultimately, it is an issue that will continue to persist into the future and one that needs greater recognition on the types and severity of harms sustained by victims," she states. "[It also] requires more holistic support to assist in recovery and help victims move forward as best they can."

your software is unable to run a scan. In these cases, get an adult involved because your computer will need to be evaluated manually.

Change your password. One of the first things you need to do if you have been hacked is to change your password. If you reused this password on other accounts, then you need to change them, too. Keep in mind that it is a very bad idea to use the same password on all your accounts. Once a hacker has your password to one account, he or she has access to everything else as well. You are making it too easy for hackers when you reuse passwords.

Delete sensitive data from the hacked account. If you can still access the hacked account, you need to go in and delete or change

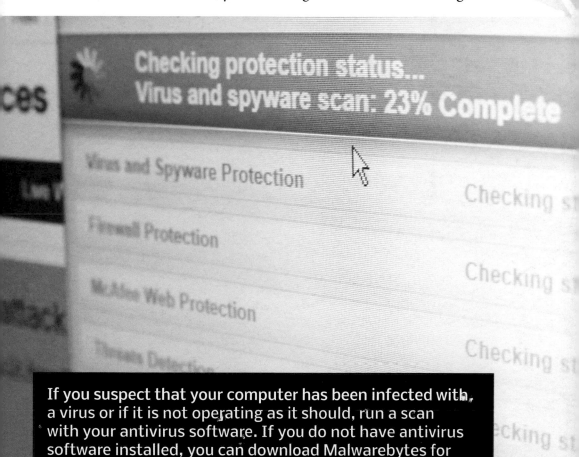

If you suspect that your computer has been infected with a virus or if it is not operating as it should, run a scan with your antivirus software. If you do not have antivirus software installed, you can download Malwarebytes for free and run a scan of your system.

any sensitive data. Such data would include things like your security questions, your credit card, or bank account numbers. You may even want to delete the hacked account altogether. The key is that you should protect your personal data as much as possible.

Check for back doors. A lot of hackers will set up a way to get back into your account even if you have successfully locked them out. For instance, they might have emails forwarded to them. Check your email filters and rules to make sure nothing is getting forwarded to another account without your knowledge. Also check to see if the security questions have changed. If your email was hacked, the hacker may be using your email as a gateway to other accounts. Be sure to update your passwords and security information on any account that has personal data.

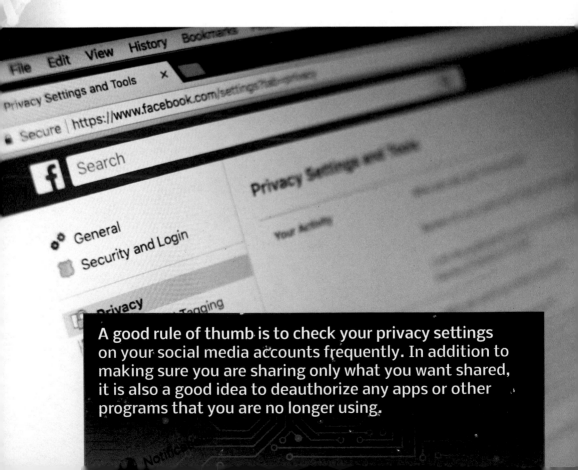

A good rule of thumb is to check your privacy settings on your social media accounts frequently. In addition to making sure you are sharing only what you want shared, it is also a good idea to deauthorize any apps or other programs that you are no longer using.

Deauthorize apps on Twitter, Facebook, and more. Anytime you take a quiz on social media, play a game, or perform some other function, you are authorizing the app to access your profile and your contact list. Be sure that you deauthorize or remove any apps from your accounts. The hacker could have used these apps as a way to get into your accounts, or, at the very least, used the app to mine data.

Tell your friends what happened. Many times, when an email gets hacked, the cybercriminals will simply use it to reach out to your contacts. For instance, they might use your account to request money or assistance. Let your friends and family know that you have been hacked. You also want to raise awareness about the potential of their being hacked.

What the Future Holds for Internet Security

Behind every new hack and behind every hole in security, there is a company or organization scrambling to stop the leak. But the problem is, there are not enough cybersecurity experts out there to help. In the next five years, experts predict that there will be a worldwide shortage of cybersecurity professionals, says Cynthia McFadden in a 2018 report for NBC's show *Today*. With so much of people's lives taking place on the internet, something needs to be done to protect them and their information.

According to the *Today* report, army Lientenant General Paul Nakasone, the head of US Cyber Command, a part of the Department of Defense (DoD), is prioritizing the recruiting of cybersecurity professionals. One way he is doing that is through a program called CyberPatriot, which teaches high school and middle school students techniques on how to defend America from cyberattacks. The program, which was started a decade ago, has grown from a handful of students in Florida to more than twenty-five thousand across the country, McFadden says in her report.

Jay Gerhinger, an adviser to North Hollywood High School's CyberPatriot program, says in Paulina Cachero's 2018 report on NBC News, Los Angeles, that there is nothing more important than a strong cyberdefense. "Our lives are on the internet these days and on the computer," he says. "Not having good cyber security is like leaving your home every day not only with the doors [unlocked], but with them wide open. There are just bad people in the world that are going to take advantage of you and we need to make sure they don't."

The Future of the Internet

Nearly 2.5 billion people have embraced the internet in its first twenty years, writes David Gorodyansky, co-owner of the software company AnchorFree, in *Wired*. "[It] is easily one of the most democratic and disruptive inventions of the last century ... (more people in the world have access to cell phones than toilets, according to the U.N.)," he continues.

As a result, to make the online world more secure, more attention is going to have to be focused on protecting data. And it needs to happen now. According to Gorodyansky, there are two things that will occur by 2020 that will impact internet security. The first is that the next five billion people will come online, the majority of whom will be from developing countries. The second, according to Gorodyansky, is that the amount of data stored online is going to grow by leaps and bounds, especially with the internet of things (IoT). The IoT refers to things that connect to the internet, such as wearable technology.

Students compete in the CyberPatriot program. The program's goal is to prepare the next generation of cybersecurity professionals.

Consequently, cybersecurity and privacy protection will become even more necessary as everything—and everyone—goes digital. To

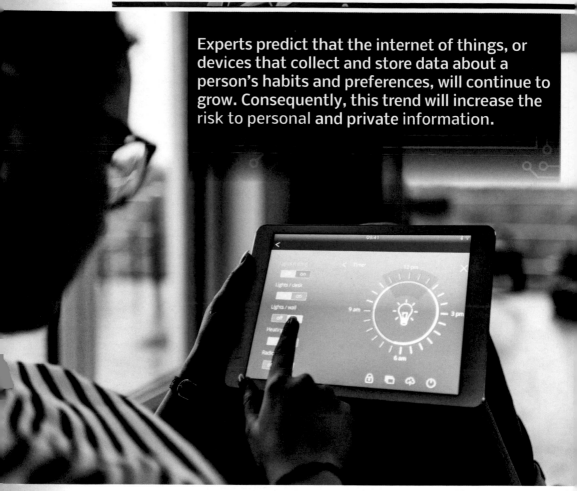

Experts predict that the internet of things, or devices that collect and store data about a person's habits and preferences, will continue to grow. Consequently, this trend will increase the risk to personal and private information.

keep all this new data safe, cybersecurity professionals will need to discover ways to protect data that can be incorporated effortlessly into daily life.

What About the Internet of Things?

The internet of things (IoT) is the concept of connecting any device to the internet. Examples include everything from headphones and other wearable devices, to coffee makers, washing machines, and home security systems. Most experts estimate that the number of

2016 US Election Experienced Russian Cyberattack

Jeanette Manfra, assistant secretary for cybersecurity and communications at the Department of Homeland Security, told NBC News in February 2018 that the Russian government had targeted state election systems during the 2016 US presidential election. "We saw a targeting of 21 states and an exceptionally small number of them were actually successfully penetrated," Manfra says.

However, she was unable to say whether the Russian government changed any state voting registration databases or undermined real votes because that was classified information. She did confirm that there is "no doubt" among US cybersecurity experts that the Russian government perpetrated these cyberattacks.

Meanwhile, cybersecurity professionals fear that this sort of cyberattack is just the beginning of Russian interference and that the United States could experience additional meddling. They are urging the US government to take steps to stop future attacks.

"All of our national security witnesses have warned that [Russia is] coming after us [again] with more election interference," declared Democratic senator Sheldon Whitehouse in the Senate in February 2018, according to Brennan Weiss of Business Insider. "And yet what have we done?"

things connected to the internet is going to increase dramatically. In fact, Gartner, an analyst firm, estimates that by 2020 there will be more than twenty-six billion connected devices. Some experts even predict this number will be more than one hundred billion. That's a lot of things connected to the internet, which represents countless opportunities for data to be stolen.

One vulnerability for data breaches could be in the use of artificial intelligence and machine learning. For instance, every "thing" you use is programmed to store data about your patterns and preferences. Whether it is your coffee maker or your voice-controlled thermostat, these devices are programmed to collect data from you. This data is then stored and used to help the machine learn more about you and adjust itself accordingly. Because this data is being stored, whether in the cloud or someplace else, it will be vulnerable to hacking.

Smart home devices like Alexa can pose privacy challenges, such as eavesdropping.

Security Threats of the Future

Right now, people live in a very interconnected world, but this connectivity is going to expand tremendously over the next ten to twenty years. For example, in the future, more decisions will be automated. People's lives might be even more reliant on virtual assistants like Siri, Google Assistant, and Alexa. People may even have connected cars that make commuting to work and school easy. Consequently, all personal data will reside in cloud computing—where people don't have control over the flow of data or access to this information. This situation, in turn, makes individuals even more vulnerable to data breaches and cybersecurity risks.

Experts, such as Gil Shwed, founder and CEO of Check Point Software Technologies, predict that people will see a number of different types of attacks in the future. In *Forbes* in September 2017, Shwed says criminals will continue to look for ways to make money off of cyberattacks; and terrorist groups will start to use cyberspace more frequently. Meanwhile, hacktivists—people who hack into organizations or groups to convey a message—will use cyberspace for their activism. There will even be people who just want to show off their hacking skills by causing data breaches.

Even governments will develop more cyberattack technologies for defense and offense. But the challenge, Shwed says, will be that, unlike in the physical world, where people know who their potential adversaries are and what weapons they use, in cyberspace, anyone can be an enemy. Furthermore, through cyberspace the United States is now accessible from every point of the globe.

Finally, the number of cyberattacks that arc run automatically by bots will increase. These bots will scan an entire network, find the weakest point, and gain entry. Therefore, companies, organizations, and even governments do not have to look weak, they simply need a vulnerable point.

Gil Shwed, founder and CEO of Check Point Software Technologies, warns that companies are often lagging behind when it comes to cybersecurity measures. In a February 2018 presentation, he said some companies are thirty years behind where they should be.

In response to this issue, experts expect to see smarter, more sophisticated ways to handle and protect large amounts of data. Some examples might include systems that can update themselves rapidly and make decisions in real time. These systems also might connect to shared-intelligence centers that work to keep information safe. The key will be developing systems that can respond to attacks quickly, shutting down any potential data leaks. All this information will be difficult for humans to handle. Therefore, they will likely rely on artificial intelligence in making decisions. There will be a growing need for cybersecurity specialists as well.

"As far as the general public is concerned, I believe that keeping ourselves cyber secure will become as commonplace as maintaining our physical safety," states Shwed in Forbes. "If today we all know to lock our doors at night, put on our seatbelts when driving, and use a helmet when hopping on our motorbikes, in ten years from now the same level of awareness will be given to ensure we are also digitally secure."

antivirus software A program designed to prevent, detect, and remove viruses and other malicious software from a computer or other device.

astute Being smart, clever, or shrewd.

bot An automated program that runs over the internet.

botnet Computers, known as zombies, that are linked together by malware.

clickbait Content on the internet designed to attract attention and entice visitors to click on a link to a particular website or article.

cloud computing Servers on the internet used to store and manage data; it is often used to save documents, photos, and other materials instead of saving them on a personal computer.

computer viruses Code that is capable of copying itself; they usually are very damaging and can corrupt computer systems or destroy data.

cookies Messages that web servers pass on to your browser when you visit a site on the internet.

data mining The process of looking for patterns in large sets of data to predict behaviors, preferences, and outcomes.

deauthorize To take back permission or consent to have access to something.

drive-by websites Websites where simply loading the page infects your computer.

encryption The process of converting information from readable data to an encoded version so that another entity cannot read it or access it.

firewall A part of a computer or network designed to block unauthorized users or systems while still allowing the computer or network to send outgoing communication.

hacker A person who uses computing skills and other tools to gain unauthorized access to computers and data.

hacktivist A hacker whose activity in gaining access to computer systems, websites, and other entities is aimed at promoting a political or social cause.

identity theft Using a person's private information and pretending to be that person, usually for financial gain.

intellectual property An invention, idea, manuscript, song, artwork, and so forth that is the product of a person's creativity and to which that person has rights.

internet of things (IoT) A description of the connection between the internet and various things or everyday objects; this connection allows the devices to send and receive data.

IP address An abbreviation for internet protocol address, the unique series of numbers that identifies each computer on the internet.

malware Software that is created to damage a computer or its systems.

multifactor authentication A security system that requires more than one way to verify a user's identity before allowing access to an account or to make a transaction.

phishing Sending emails pretending to be a reputable company to convince individuals to share personal information, such as passwords and credit card numbers.

ransomware Malicious software that keeps users from accessing their computer until a sum of money is paid.

social engineering The art of manipulating people into sharing personal information.

Trojan horse A computer virus or malware that, when activated, can take control of a computer and steal or harm data files.

URL The abbreviation for "uniform resource locater" and the address for a web page.

World Wide Web An information system on the internet that allows people to share information.

zombie A computer that is linked to the internet and that has been taken over by malware, viruses, or worms. A group or network of zombies is called a botnet.

Center for Internet Security (CIS)

31 Tech Valley Drive, #2
East Greenbush, NY 12061
(518) 266-3460
Website: https://www.cisecurity.org
Facebook: @CenterforIntSec
Twitter: @CISecurity

CIS is a nonprofit organization dedicated to achieving cybersecurity readiness for both the public and private sectors. It also provides resources that help people achieve security goals.

Get Cyber Safe

Department of Public Safety and Emergency Preparedness
Minister of Public Safety
House of Commons
Ottawa, ON K1A 0A6
Canada
(613) 991-0657
Website: https://www.getcybersafe.gc.ca/index-en.aspx
Facebook and Twitter: @GetCyberSafe
Instagram: @getcybersafe

A national public awareness campaign, Get Cyber Safe was created to educate Canadians about internet security. The organization also provides information on steps people can take to protect themselves online.

Internet Security Alliance

2500 Wilson Boulevard, #245
Arlington, VA 22201
(703) 907-7090
Website: https://isalliance.org
Twitter: @ISAlliance

The Internet Security Alliance was founded in 2000 in connection with Carnegie Mellon University. The group's mission is to combine technology and public policy to create innovative and effective cybersecurity programs that will stand the test of time.

Media Smarts

205 Catherine Street, Suite 100
Ottawa, ON K2P 1C3
Canada
(800) 896-3342
Website: http://mediasmarts.ca
Facebook and Twitter: @MediaSmarts

This organization has been developing digital and media literacy programs for Canadian homes, schools, and communities since 1996. Their work falls into three primary areas: education, research and policy, and public awareness.

SANS Institute

11200 Rockville Pike, Suite 200
North Bethesda, MD 20852
(301) 654-7267
Website: https://www.sans.org
Facebook: @SANS.EDU
Twitter: @SANSInstitute

SANS is the most trusted source for information security training and certification in the world. The organization also develops, maintains, and makes available at no cost, research documents about various aspects of information security. It also operates the internet's early warning system—the Internet Storm Center.

Stay Safe Online

National Cyber Security Alliance (NCSA)
1010 Vermont Avenue NW
Washington, DC 2005
(956) 234-6938
Website: https://staysafeonline.org
Facebook and Twitter: @staysafeonline

Stay Safe Online is the initiative of the NCSA to educate and empower the digital community to use the internet safely and securely. They also strive to ensure that the technology people use and the networks they connect with are protected.

For Further Reading

Abramovitz, Melissa. *Cybersecurity Analyst* (Cutting Edge Careers). San Diego, CA: ReferencePoint Press, Inc., 2018.

Eboch, M. M. *Data Mining* (Introducing Issues with Opposing Viewpoints). New York, NY: Greenhaven Press, 2018.

Ells, June. *Teens Avoiding Predators Online* (Teen CyberSmarts: Staying Safe Online). Interactive ebook. New York, NY: Rosen Publishing, 2014.

Ells, June. *Teens Protecting Their Privacy Online* (Teen CyberSmarts: Staying Safe Online). Interactive ebook. New York, NY: Rosen Publishing, 2014.

Ells, June. *Teens Using Social Networks* (Teen CyberSmarts: Staying Safe Online). Interactive ebook. New York, NY: Rosen Publishing, 2014.

Fromm, Megan. *Privacy and Digital Security* (Media Literacy). New York, NY: Rosen Publishing, 2015.

Higgins, Melissa, and Michael Regan. *Cybersecurity* (Special Reports). Edina, MN: Essential Library, 2015.

Kamberg, Mary-Lane. *Cybersecurity: Protecting Your Identity and Data* (Digital and Information Library). New York, NY: Rosen Publishing, 2018.

Orr, Tamra. *Digital Privacy: Securing Your Data* (Digital Citizenship and You). New York, NY: Rosen Publishing, 2019.

Wilkinson, Colin. *Everything You Need to Know About Digital Privacy* (The Need to Know Library). New York, NY: Rosen Publishing, 2018.

Bibliography

Botelho, Greg. "Arrest Made in Miss Teen USA Cassidy Wolf 'Sextortion Case.'" CNN, September 26, 2013. https://www.cnn.com/2013/09/26/justice/miss-teen-usa-sextortion/index.html.

Cachero, Paulina. "North Hollywood High CyberPatriots Aim to Defend Cyber Security Title." NBC Los Angeles, April 9, 2018. https://www.nbclosangeles.com/news/local/North-Hollywood-High-CyberPatriots-Cyber-Security-Champions-479179963.html.

Chappell, Robert P. Jr. *Child Identity Theft: What Every Parent Needs to Know*. Lanham, MD: Rowman & Littlefield, 2018.

CompTIA. "Organizations Changing Strategies and Tactics as Security Environment Gets More Complex, New CompTIA Study Finds." March 31, 2015. https://www.comptia.org/about-us/newsroom/press-releases/2015/03/31/organizations-changing-strategies-and-tactics-as-security-environment-gets-more-complex-new-comptia-study-finds.

Finger, David. "Closing the Book on the 2011 Sony Playstation Data Breach." CSO Online, June 19, 2014. https://www.csoonline.com/article/2365307/data-breach/closing-the-book-on-the-2011-sony-playstation-data-breach.html.

Forbes. "What Will Cybersecurity Look Like 10 Years from Now?" September 14, 2017. https://www.forbes.com.

Gaudiosi, John. "Why Sony Didn't Learn from Its 2011 Attack." *Fortune*, December 24, 2014. http://fortune.com/2014/12/24/why-sony-didnt-learn-from-its-2011-hack.

Gebhart, Gennie. *Spying on Students: School-Issued Devices and Student Privacy*. Electronic Frontier Foundation, April 13, 2017. https://www.eff.org/wp/school-issued-devices-and-student-privacy#conclusion.

Gorodyansky, David. "Privacy and Security in the Internet Age." *Wired*. Retrieved September 12, 2018. https://www.wired.com.

Honan, Matt. "What to Do After You've Been Hacked." *Wired*, March 5, 2013. https://www.wired.com.

Kauflin, Jeff. "The Fast-Growing Job with a Huge Skills Gap: Cyber Security." *Forbes*, March 16, 2017. https://www.forbes.com/sites/jeffkauflin/2017/03/16/the-fast-growing-job-with-a-huge-skills-gap-cyber-security/#5d8bf3a75163.

Klein, Rebecca. "Lawsuit Alleges that Google Has Crossed a Creepy Line with Student Data." Huffington Post, March 17, 2014. https://www.huffingtonpost.com/2014/03/17/google-data-mining-students_n_4980422.html.

Kobie, Nicole. "The Emotional Burden of Being Hacked." Motherboard, December 4, 2017. https://motherboard.vice.com/en_us/article/8xm4mv/the-emotional-burden-of-being-hacked-stressweek2017.

Lardinois, Frederic. "Google Says Its G Suite for Education Now Has 70M Users." Tech Crunch, January 24, 2017. https://techcrunch.com/2017/01/24/google-says-its-g-suite-for-education-now-has-70m-users.

Madden, Mary, and Rainie, Lee. "Americans' Attitudes About Privacy, Security and Surveillance." Pew Research Center, May 20, 2015. http://www.pewinternet.org/2015/05/20/americans-attitudes-about-privacy-security-and-surveillance.

McElhearn, Kirk. "8 Things to Do Right Now if You've Been Hacked." Intego, October 26, 2016. https://www.intego.com.

McFadden, Cynthia. "Meet the Teens Groomed as the Future of Cyber Security." *Today*, June 29, 2018. https://www.today.com/video/meet-the-teens-being-groomed-as-the-future-of-cyber-security-1266828355756?v=railb.

McFadden, Cynthia, et al. "Russians Penetrated U.S. Voter Systems Top U.S. Official Says." *NBC News*, updated February 8, 2018. https://www.nbcnews.com/politics/elections/russians -penetrated-u-s-voter-systems-says-top-u-s-n845721.

Media Smarts Canada. "Cyber Security Consumer Tip Sheet: Safe Surfing." Retrieved September 11, 2018. http://mediasmarts .ca/tipsheet/cyber-security-consumer-tip-sheet-safe-surfing.

Media Smarts Canada. "Cyber Security: Special Issues for Teens." Retrieved September 11, 2018. http://mediasmarts.ca/cyber -security/cyber-security-special-issues-teens.

Morgan, Jacob. "A Simple Explanation of the Internet of Things." *Forbes*, May 13, 2014. https://www.forbes.com/sites /jacobmorgan/2014/05/13/simple-explanation-internet -things-that-anyone-can-understand/#216223241d09.

Phillips, Tom. "Five Years Ago Today, Sony Admitted the Great PSN Attack," Eurogamer, April 26, 2016. https://www .eurogamer.net.

Rashid, Fahmida Y. "Myth 1: I Will Know When I Am Infected (93 Perent)." *eWeek*, June 28, 2011. http://www.eweek.com /security/myth-1-i-will-know-when-i-am-infected-93-percent.

Ravenscraft, Eric. "It's No Surprise Anymore: Your Data Is Never Safe Online." Lifehacker, November 26, 2013. https://lifehacker. com/its-no-surprise-anymore-your-data-is-never-safe -onlin-1471858210.

Rubenking, Neil J. "What to Do When You've Been Hacked." *PCMag*, September 12, 2017. https://www.pcmag.com.

Saito, William H. "These Are 10 Cybersecurity Myths That Must Be Busted." *Forbes*, April 4, 2017. https://www.forbes.com/sites /williamsaito/2017/04/04/these-are-10-cybersecurity-myths -that-must-be-busted.

Scheff, Sue. "Google Apps for Education: Data Mining and the Threat to Student Privacy," Huffington Post, April 9, 2014. https://www.huffingtonpost.com.

Steinberg, Joseph. "14 Signs Your Smartphone or Tablet Has Been Hacked." *Inc.*, November 1, 2016. https://www.inc.com.

Steinberg, Joseph. "Massive Security Breach at Sony—Here's What You Need to Know." *Forbes*, December 11, 2014. https://www.forbes.com/sites/josephsteinberg/2014/12/11/massive-security-breach-at-sony-heres-what-you-need-to-know/#305d393944d8.

Symantec Corporation. "5 Predictions on the Future of the Internet of Things." Retrieved September 11, 2018. https://us.norton.com/internetsecurity-iot-5-predictions-for-the-future-of-iot.html.

Verizon Wireless. "2018 Data Breach Investigations Report." Retrieved September 12, 2018. https://www.verizonenterprise.com/verizon-insights-lab/dbir.

Weiss, Brennan. "Top American Cyber Official Says Russia 'Successfully Penetrated' Some US Voter Systems During 2016 Election." Business Insider, February 8, 2018. https://www.businessinsider.com.

Wolf, Cassidy. "Miss Teen USA Lived Through Your Worst Hacking Nightmare—Hear Her Frightening Story." Teen Vogue, November 8, 2013. https://www.teenvogue.com/story/cassidy-wolf-hacking.

Zaidiner, Yana. "Five Easy Habits to Keep Your Data Safe." *Forbes*, June 26, 2016. https://www.forbes.com.

Index

A

Abrahams, Jared James, 16
Alexa, 47
AnchorFree, 43
antivirus software, 12, 25, 37
application-layer attacks, 22
artificial intelligence, 46

B

back doors, 40
botnet, 26, 47

C

Chappell, Robert, 9
Check Point Software
    Technologies, 47
clickbait, 32
cookies, 29–30
Cross, Cassandra, 38
CyberPatriot, 42

D

data breaches, 6, 8, 12, 18, 20,
    27, 35, 37, 38, 46, 47
data mining, 4, 22, 28, 41
deauthorizing apps, 41
denial of service (DoS) attacks,
    21–22
Department of Defense
    (DoD), 42

Department of Homeland
    Security, 45
directed threats, 13–14
distributed denial of service
    (DDoS) attacks, 21–22
drive-by website, 13

E

eavesdropping, 20–21
Electronic Frontier Foundation
    (EFF), 28–29
emotional repercussions of
    hacking, 38
encryption, 20, 25
exploiting attacks, 22

F

fake news, 32
Federal Bureau of Investigation
    (FBI), 16
firewall, 13, 29

G

Gartner, 46
Gebhart, Gennie, 29
Gerhinger, Jay, 42
Google, 11, 28–29, 47
Gorodyansky, David, 43
G Suite for Education, 28–29

H

hacktivists, 47

hotspots, 27–28
https, 25

I
identity theft, 6, 9–10, 15, 22
internet of things (IoT), 43, 44, 46
internet security
  definition, 9–11
  future threats, 47–49
  how breaches occur, 20–22
  importance of, 17–19
  methods of protection, 24–33
  responding to attacks, 37–41
  signs of attack, 34–37
  types of threats, 11–15
IP address spoofing, 22

K
Kobie, Nicole, 38

L
Lawrence, Jennifer, 38

M
machine learning, 46
malware, 9, 14, 16, 17, 25, 34, 36, 37
Malwarebytes, 37
Manfra, Jeanette, 45
McFadden, Cynthia, 42
mental health, 38

Miliefsky, Gary, 8
multifactor authentication, 33

N
Nakasone, Paul, 42
Norton, 38

P
password attacks, 22
personally identifying information (PII), 29
phishing, 8, 9, 13, 14, 20, 31, 37
PlayStation Network (PSN), 6–8
pop-ups, 34, 36
privacy tools, 31
proxying, 37

R
ransomware, 9, 12
Ravenscraft, Eric, 15
Rubin, Julia, 16
Russian cyberattack, 45

S
Shwed, Gil, 47–49
Siri, 47
Snopes, 33
social engineering, 20
Sony, 6–8
Steinberg, Joseph, 8
strong passwords, 13, 22, 27, 31

Symantec, 18
system updates, 25, 30

T
terrorists, 47

U
undirected threats, 13

V
viruses, 9, 12, 13, 20, 22, 35, 37

W
Ward, Lewis, 8
Whitehouse, Sheldon, 45
Wolf, Cassidy, 16–17, 22–23

Z
zombie computer, 22

About the Author

Sherri Mabry Gordon is a bullying prevention advocate and author. Many of her books deal with issues teens face today, including bullying, abuse, public shaming, online safety, and more. Gordon also writes about bullying, relationships, and online safety for Verywell.com. She has given multiple presentations to schools, churches, and the YMCA on bullying prevention, dating abuse, and online safety and volunteers regularly. She also serves on the School Counselor Advisory Board for two schools. Gordon resides in Columbus, Ohio, with her husband and two children.

Photo Credits